Fetch!

BOXERS

Valerie Bodden

Creative Education • Creative Paperbacks

published by Creative Education and Creative Paperbacks
P.O. Box 227, Mankato, Minnesota 56002
Creative Education and Creative Paperbacks are imprints of
The Creative Company
www.thecreativecompany.us

design and production by Christine Vanderbeek
art direction by Rita Marshall
printed in the United States of America

photographs by Alamy (Charlotta Fredriksson, Moviestore
collection Ltd), Dreamstime (Robseguin, Stanislav Tolubaev),
Getty Images (Neilson Barnard/USA Network/NBCU), iS-
tockphoto (baratroli, fotojagodka, rusm, tshortell, utkaman-
darinka), Shutterstock (Utekhina Anna, Hugo Felix, GoDog
Photo, Eric Isselee, Jagodka, Erik Lam, Neveshkin Nikolay,
otsphoto, PhotocechCZ, rebeccaashworth, Scorpp, Viorel
Sima, Nikolai Tsvetkov, Lebedinski Vladislav, WilleeCole
Photography, Dora Zett)

library of congress cataloging-in-publication data
Names: Bodden, Valerie, author.
Title: Boxers / Valerie Bodden.
Series: Fetch!
Includes bibliographical references and index.
Summary: A brief overview of the physical characteristics,
personality traits, and habits of the boxer breed, as well as
descriptions of famous pop-culture boxers such as Wilson.
Identifiers:
ISBN 978-1-60818-897-0 (hardcover)
ISBN 978-1-62832-513-3 (pbk)
ISBN 978-1-56660-949-4 (eBook)
This title has been submitted for CIP processing under
LCCN 2017938922.
CCSS: RI.1.1, 2, 4, 5, 6, 7; RI.2.1, 2, 5, 6, 7;
RI.3.1, 5, 7; RF.1.1, 3, 4; RF.2.3, 4

first edition HC 9 8 7 6 5 4 3 2 1
first edition PBK 9 8 7 6 5 4 3 2 1

TABLE OF CONTENTS

Fetch!

BOXING BOXERS

A boxer is a *breed* of dog. Boxers are smart and friendly. They love to goof around. Sometimes they put up their front feet when they play. They look like they are boxing!

Fetch!

WHAT DO BOXERS LOOK LIKE?

Boxers have muscular bodies. They have square heads with a wrinkly forehead. Their eyes are big and brown. Many have *erect* ears. Others have ears that hang down. Most boxers have *docked* tails.

Many boxers have markings on the face, called a mask.

Boxers are about two feet (0.6 m) tall. Females weigh 50 to 65 pounds (22.7–29.5 kg). Males weigh 65 to 80 pounds (29.5–36.3 kg). Boxers have short, shiny fur. It can be tan, white, or brown with white or black markings.

BOXER PUPPIES

Newborn boxer puppies weigh about one pound (0.5 kg). They grow quickly. But boxers will act like playful puppies until they are two or three years old.

Mother boxers usually have five to seven puppies.

Fetch!

BOXERS ON THE SCREEN

Boxers can be seen on TV. In the cartoon *Pound Puppies*, Cookie is a boxer. Cookie is smart and tough. She helps puppies find new homes. Boxers have also starred in **commercials** (*cuh-MUR-shulz*) for shoes and cars.

Curious boxers are smart; they learn new commands quickly.

· 13 ·

Fetch!

BOXERS AND PEOPLE

More than 100 years ago, people used boxers to herd cattle. Boxers were also some of the first police dogs. Some boxers served in wars, too. They helped find hurt soldiers. Today, many boxers work as search-and-rescue dogs. Boxers also make good *therapy dogs*.

Boxers in dog shows (right) usually have erect ears and docked tails.

Boxers are very good with kids. Both puppies and adults make good pets. Puppies have a lot of energy. Adults can be calmer. They learn quickly. Some people think male boxers are sweeter than females.

Though they are spirited dogs, boxers can also be patient.

WHAT DO BOXERS LIKE TO DO?

Boxers like to spend time with their family. They need to live indoors. Boxers cannot stay outside too long in the hot or cold. But they do need to exercise every day.

Boxers like to run and spend time with other dogs.

Boxers love to learn new tricks. Teach your dog to run through tunnels and leap over jumps. You will both have fun!

A FAMOUS BOXER

The dog Wilson from the 2003 movie *Good Boy!* is a playful, funny boxer. In the movie, a boy named Owen can talk to dogs. When Wilson finds out, he asks for a cookie. Then he asks for 20 cookies. Wilson helps save Earth from alien dogs who try to take over the planet.

GLOSSARY

breed a kind of an animal with certain traits, such as long ears or a good nose

commercials short ads meant to make people want to buy a product

docked made shorter by cutting off the end

erect standing upright

therapy dogs dogs that help people who are sick or hurt by letting the people pet and enjoy them

READ MORE

Heos, Bridget. *Do You Really Want a Dog?* North Mankato, Minn.: Amicus, 2014.

Johnson, Jinny. *Boxer*. North Mankato, Minn.: Smart Apple Media, 2013.

Schuh, Mari. *Boxers*. Minneapolis: Bellwether Media, 2016.

WEBSITES

American Kennel Club: Boxer
http://www.akc.org/dog-breeds/boxer/
Learn more about boxers, and check out lots of boxer pictures.

Bailey's Responsible Dog Owner's Coloring Book
http://classic.akc.org/pdfs/public_education/coloring_book.pdf
Print out pictures to color, and learn more about caring for a pet dog.

Every effort has been made to ensure that these sites are suitable for children, that they have educational value, and that they contain no inappropriate material. However, because of the nature of the Internet, it is impossible to guarantee that these sites will remain active indefinitely or that their contents will not be altered.

INDEX